Contents

Mike Wilson

Published in association with The Basic Skills Agency

A MEMBER OF THE HODDER HEADLINE GROUP

The Publishers would like to thank the following for permission to reproduce copyright material:

Photo credits
p.4 © AFP/Getty Images; p.15 © POPPERFOTO/Alamy; p.21 Lars Baron/Bongarts/Getty Images; p.26 © John Peters/Manchester United via Getty Images.
Every effort has been made to trace all copyright holders, but if any have been inadvertently overlooked the Publishers will be pleased to make the necessary arrangements at the first opportunity.

Orders: please contact Bookpoint Ltd, 130 Milton Park, Abingdon, Oxon OX14 4SB. Telephone: (44) 01235 827720. Fax: (44) 01235 400454. Lines are open 9.00 - 6.00, Monday to Saturday, with a 24-hour message answering service. Visit our website at www.hoddereducation.co.uk

© Mike Wilson, 2006
First published in 2006 by
Hodder Murray, an imprint of Hodder Education,
a member of the Hodder Headline Group
338 Euston Road
London NW1 3BH

Impression number   10 9 8 7 6 5 4 3 2 1
Year   2011 2010 2009 2008 2007 2006

Illustrations © Barking Dog Art.
Cover photos: main © Aflo Foto Agency/Alamy; top left © Royalty-Free/Corbis; bottom left © POPPERFOTO/Alamy.
Typeset by SX Composing DTP, Rayleigh, Essex.
Printed in Great Britain by CPI, Bath

A catalogue record for this title is available from the British Library

ISBN-10: 0 340 91547 1
ISBN-13: 978 0 340 91547 9

It's Only a Game!

Go to any country in the world.
You will see people playing football.

What makes us do it?
What makes us want to kick a ball
between two sticks?

What makes us want to stand
and watch other people kick a ball
between two sticks?

Bill Shankly knew the answer.
He was manager of Liverpool
in the 1970s.
Bill Shankly said:

'People say football is life and death.
But it's not.
It's much more important than that!'

Early Days

Seven hundred years ago,
King Edward III banned football.

This was not the football we play today.
The goals were the gates of a church,
or the wall of a big house.
One goal was in one village,
the other goal in the next village.

There were no rules.
You could throw the ball, carry it or kick it.
You could even kick the other players.

You could punch, push, bite and fight.
So long as you got the ball
to the goal in the next village!

That's why the king had to ban football.
Too many men had been killed.
The rest were not fit to go to war!

Two hundred years ago,
football was mainly played in public schools –
places like Eton, Harrow and Rugby.

It was still a mad free-for-all,
and people still got hurt.

Then one day in 1823,
a Rugby schoolboy, William Webb Ellis,
picked up the ball and ran with it.
Some players said he was cheating.
From that day, two different games –
football and rugby – began to split apart.

In 1863, the rules of football
were set down for the first time.
You could stop the ball with your hand.
But you could not carry it or throw it.
Nor could you grab, kick or hit other players.
Other rules, like
- the size of the pitch,
- the size of the goals and
- the number of men in each team,
were not sorted until a few years later!

Football Academy

Dear Sir

I love football.
I want to play football when I grow up.

I want to be like Wayne Rooney.
I know he went to a Football Academy
when he was a boy.

How can I join a Football Academy?
How can I join a top club?
What is a Football Academy like?

Yours faithfully
Mark

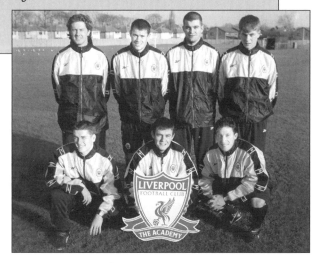

Dear Mark

Wayne Rooney is not the only star
who went to a Football Academy.
Steven Gerrard, Michael Owen,
David Beckham, Paul Scholes . . .
They all started in a Football Academy.

All of the big clubs have an Academy.
You have to be spotted by a talent scout.
Or you can ask for a trial.

Some places take boys and girls.
They take kids from the age of eight or nine.

There are one-day courses in school-time,
and five-day courses in the holidays.
You will learn about:
  • football fitness
  • healthy eating and healthy living
  • football skills
  • football tactics.

And you get to play a lot of football!

Football Tactics

Until the 1920s,
players formed up in
an M and a W shape.

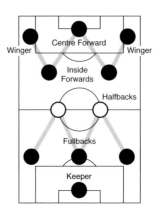

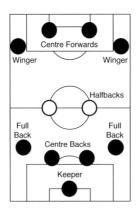

Then the offside laws changed.
It was easier to score goals.
Teams began playing a 4–2–4 shape.
This kept more players at the back.

In 1953, England played Hungary at Wembley.
Hungary's tactics left England standing.
The players moved round, and changed places.
The centre forward played deep in midfield.
England's man-for-man marking fell apart.

England lost 6–3, their first ever defeat at home.

A year later, they met again – in Hungary.
Hungary won again: 7–1!
That was England's worst defeat ever!

In the 1970s and 1980s,
Holland played football like Hungary.
They called it **Total Football**.

Strikers would drop back into midfield.
Midfielders would push up to join the attack.
Left back and right back became wing backs.
They would attack like old-fashioned wingers.

Total Football changed the game.
It's a tactic you can still see in football today.

Other shapes have been tried over the years:

- 4–3–3 (This is how England won the World Cup in 1966.)

- 3–5–2 (is good for packing the midfield).

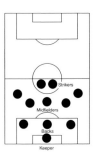

- England even tried a weird 4–3–2–1 shape, called the Christmas Tree. (But it didn't last long!)

- Most teams today go for 4–4–2.

Football tactics can lead to crazy results.

It was the end of the season, 1898.
If Stoke and Burnley drew 0–0,
they'd both stay up in the First Division.
So they made sure they drew 0–0.
There was not a single shot at goal!

- In Yugoslavia in 1979, it was a different story.
  One side would get promotion
  if they won by a lot of goals.
  The other team let them win 134–1!
  That's a goal every 40 seconds!

- In one game in Argentina,
  one team went on strike.
  Their tactics were
  to sit down on the pitch and not play.
  They lost 71–0!

Football Question and Answer

Q: Which was the first English club
to play a match with no English players
in the team?

A: Chelsea, in December 1999.

Q: Which was the last club to play a match
with only English players in the team?

A: Spurs, in December 2000.

Q: How much does a
famous football shirt cost?

A: In 2002, Pelé's famous No 10 shirt
from the 1970 World Cup Final
was sold for a record £157,000.

Q: Who wants to eat David Beckham?

A: Fans in Japan. Hundreds went to see
a giant statue of David Beckham.
The statue was made of chocolate!

Q: Name two famous World Cup crimes.

A: In 1966, just before the Final at Wembley, the World Cup was stolen.
It was found in a garden, three days later, by a dog named Pickles.

A: In the 1986 World Cup,
England were playing Argentina.
Maradona jumped for the ball
with the England goalie.
Maradona hit it into the net with his hand.
The ref didn't see the handball.
Later, Maradona said he didn't do it.
He said it was 'the Hand of God'.

Q: Which team has won the most FA Cup Finals?

A: Manchester United.
They have been in 16 finals
and won 11 of them.
Arsenal have been in 16 finals,
but won only 10 of them.

Here are some trick questions.

Q: How come Gary Lineker said:
'Football is a game of four halves'?

A: In some competitions,
you play two matches – home and away.

Q: In 1971, Rangers played Lisbon.
The score was 6–6 after extra time.
Rangers lost a penalty shoot-out 3–0,
yet they still won the match. How come?

A: The ref made a mistake.
Rangers had scored more away goals,
so they didn't need the penalty shoot-out.
The ref was sacked
and Rangers went on to the next round!

Q: Which team won the FA Cup
and never scored a goal?
(This is a trick question
 with two trick answers.)

A: Cardiff won 1–0 in 1927 –
the other team scored an own goal!
And back in 1871 a team won when
a player called Willie Never scored!

(Take your pick!)

'Football is War'

(Rinus Michels, Holland Coach 1974 to 1992)

1914 World War I. Christmas Day.

English and German soldiers stopped fighting.

They left the trenches and met in No-Man's Land.

Then they had a game of football.

1970 Two countries from Latin America,

El Salvador and Honduras,

went to war after a game of football.

El Salvador won the match 3–2.

A week later, Honduras invaded El Salvador.

El Salvador invaded Honduras.

The war lasted four days.

1970 A civil war raged in Nigeria, in Africa.

The two sides agreed to stop fighting

for two days.

They all wanted to go and watch Pelé,

the best player ever, play in a charity match!

The Best Player Ever

Pelé was the best player ever.
He was born in Brazil.

Pelé started his career at 15.
He won his first World Cup at 17.
No one has won more Championship medals.

In all, Pelé played 1,363 matches.
He scored 1,281 goals.
That's nearly a goal a match!

Here's what one player said
after he played against Pelé
in the 1970 World Cup:

'Before the game, I told myself –
he's only flesh and blood,
he's only human.
After the game, I knew I was wrong!'

Pelé holding the World Cup in 1970.

Funny but True!

In the 1940s, one team
was playing in thick fog.
After 30 minutes, the fog was so thick
the ref couldn't see what was going on.

The ref stopped the game.
The players all went in for an early bath.
Ten minutes later,
someone said, 'Where's Alf?'

They went outside, and found the goalie.
He was still standing in his goal,
trying to see into the fog!

*

In 1900, the weather was so bad
in one match that the Aston Villa team
wore overcoats and carried umbrellas!

*

Football is a game of three halves.
How come?

In one match in 1894, the ref was late.
The teams had played 45 minutes
when he got there.
He made them start the match again!

By the end, the players were tired.
They had played 135 minutes.
A game of three halves!

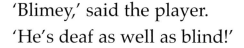

*

In one match, the ref gave a free kick.
One player shouted at the ref,
'Are you blind?'
The ref turned on him:
'WHAT DID YOU SAY?'

'Blimey,' said the player.
'He's deaf as well as blind!'

'When You Are 0-0 Down . . .'

Football quotes

Sometimes the TV experts say funny things.
Sometimes it just comes out wrong:

Apart from their goals, Norway haven't scored!

That ball had to go in! But it didn't!

*We scored the winner
two minutes from time.
But then they went and equalised!*

*That player never fails to hit the target.
But that was a miss!*

*We can go all the way to the Final . . .
Unless someone knocks us out.*

*That player dribbles a lot.
The other side don't like it.
You can see it all over their faces!*

Can We Play Too?

The women's game

In 1916, a team of women played a team of men.
The men kept their hands behind their backs
to make it fair! (The women won!)

Women's football was banned in 1921.
The men said football was not very ladylike!
But it didn't stop women playing.

It took until the 1960s to get the ban lifted.

The first Women's International
was between England and Scotland.
It was in 1972 –
exactly 100 years after the men's match!

Now there are over 100,000 women
playing football in the UK.

The Best Woman Player Ever

Birgit Prinz was born in 1977.
She has been scoring goals for Germany
since she was 17.

She was FIFA Women's Player of the Year
three years in a row – 2003, 2004 and 2005.

Birgit scored in the Final of Euro 2005.
Germany beat Norway 3–1.
They won for the fourth time in a row!

Birgit has scored in three Euro Finals:
in 1995, 1997 and 2005.

Yet she says,
'Every goal you score is a team effort.
You never score a goal just by yourself.'

Birgit Prinz (left) in action with Elisabetta Tona of Italy
during the Women's Euro 2005.

Football Facts

The biggest win in a top match

1885 In Scotland,
Arbroath beat Bon Accord 36–0.

The longest penalty shoot-out

1975 North Korea beat Hong Kong
11–10 in the Asia Cup.

It took them 28 penalties to win the match.

The youngest player

1980 Eamonn Collins played for Blackpool
in the Anglo-Scottish Cup when he was 14.

The oldest player

1965 Football legend Stanley Matthews
was still playing for Stoke when he was 50.

The biggest come-back

1957 Charlton were 5–1 down
with 30 minutes to go.

They scored six goals and won 7–6!

The fastest goal

1998 Uruguay, South America.
Ricardo Olivera shot at goal
right from the kick-off.
The goalie was off his line.
It was 1–0, after only 2.8 seconds!

The fastest sending-off

1999 Swansea playing Darlington.
Swansea had a free kick.
Walter Boyd came on as sub.
He got into a fight
before the free kick was taken.
Boyd was sent off before the game restarted!

The longest game of 'keepy-uppy'

1994 Ricardo Neves, from Brazil,
started a game of 'keepy-uppy'.
The ball didn't touch the ground
for the next 19 hours!

First £1,000 player

1905 Alf Common went
to Middlesbrough from Sunderland.

First £100,000 player

1961 Denis Law went
to Italy from Manchester City.

First £1 million player

1979 Trevor Francis went
to Nottingham Forest from Birmingham City.

Most expensive English player

2002 Rio Ferdinand went
to Manchester United from Leeds.
He cost £29 million.

Most expensive player in the world – so far

2001 Zinedine Zidane was sold to Real Madrid
for £47 million.

Who will be the NEXT
most expensive player in the world?
Is anyone worth more than £47 million?

Golden Boy

Wayne Rooney is England's 'Golden Boy'.

He scored his first goal
in his first ever proper match.
It was for a local Under-12s side.
Wayne was still only seven!

Wayne joined the Everton Academy
when he was nine years old.
He played his first full game
for Everton in October 2002.

Wayne was the youngest player
to play in the Premiership.
He was just 16 years and 360 days old.

(James Vaughan,
another Everton player,
now holds the record.
In April 2005, he was 16 years and 271 days old.)

Wayne Rooney playing for Manchester United.

In February 2003, Wayne got his first England cap.

At 17 years, he became the youngest player
to play – and score – for England.

In 2004, Manchester United bought Wayne
for a whacking £27 million.
It was money well spent,
because Wayne scored a hat-trick
in his first match!

In December 2004, Wayne was voted 'Golden Boy' –
the Best Young Player in Europe.
Then, in 2005, he was voted
UK Young Player of the Year.
He was still only 19 years old.

Football Quiz

Look carefully for the answers.
The questions may catch you out!

1 Who tried to ban football 700 years ago?

2 Who 'invented' the game of rugby
when he picked up the ball and ran with it?

3 What was the score when England
played Hungary in 1954?

4 Who is the best player ever?
Where is he from?

5 Who is the best woman player ever?
Where is she from?

6 Which team has won the FA Cup
the most times?

7 Who said, 'Football is a game of four halves'?

8 What was the name of the goalie in the fog?

9 Who is the most expensive player ever?

10 How much did he cost?